Contents

Innit *by Jackie Kay* ....
Labajada Hill *by Lomawywesa (Michael*
Clearing Out *by Geoffrey Summerfield* .
Before the Beginning *by Gareth Owen* 5
What She Did *by Roger McGough*. 6
Mistaken Identity *by John Mole* 7
A Fishy Poem *by Nikki Giovanni* 8
Visiting Rights *by Steven Herrick* 9
El Garrobo (The Lizard) *by Bosco Centeno*. 10
Voice in the Night *by Joan Poulson* 11
I Want to Forget *by The Rebel Poet-Priest of Bengal* 12
A Game of Squash *by Dick King-Smith* 13
Mary *by Elizabeth Jennings* 14
The Wedding Feast *by Julie O'Callagan* 15
So So Illogical *by Sharon Bell* 16
When *by Lee Bennett Hopkins* 17
Away Day *by Adrian Henri*. 18
Just Wait *by Valerie Bloom* 19
All You Who Sleep Tonight *by Vikram Seth*. 20
Something He Left *by Kit Wright*. 21
When I Was a Boy *by Charles Causley* 22
Ill *by Gavin Ewart* 24
The Pedlar's Caravan *by William Brighty Rands* 25
You Try to Tell Them *by Marisa Horsford* 26
Something to Worry About *by Benjamin Zephaniah* 27
Gutted *by Chrissie Gittins* 28
Jealousy *by Ian Serraillier* 29
Growing Pains *by Jean Little*. 30
Index of poem features 32

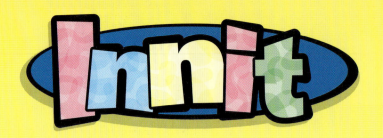

Innit he's a football star, my dad.
Innit he's got a gold car, my dad.
Innit, he dresses really bad, my dad.
Innit, his muscles are well hard, my dad.
Innit, he's got a sixpack, my dad.
Innit, he's the leader of his pack, my dad.
Innit, his flying kick is wild, my dad.
Innit, I'm his only child, my dad.
Innit, he's rich and famous, my dad.

Innit, I've been had, my dad.
Innit, I've never met him, my dad.
Innit, he's bought me nothing, my dad.
Innit, I've got his eyes, my dad.
(I hope I haven't caught his lies, my dad.)
Innit, I'm not rich and famous.
I'm not, am I? Innit? Innit? Innit?

Jackie Kay

Labajada Hill

Over Labajada Hill
Claire yells
      "My home town"
Santa Fe unfolds
before us
      "This is where I was born"
Like grandfather Kabotie
she owns a
bit of Santa Fe in her
heart as flowers unfolded
above in blue skies

Into Santa Fe
grandfather Kabotie was exiled
to become a white man
but grew
more Hopi continuing
with the sacred corn

Now Claire the third generation
Kabotie coming
to Santa Fe to
blossom another
sacred corn.

Lomawywesa
(Michael Kabotie)

Clearing out

One day my grandfather cleans out
His favourite coat's coat-pockets.

He finds three dusty peppermints
And two electric sockets,
A losing ticket for a raffle
And fifteen paper-clips,
An ointment that works wonders
When the winter cracks your lips,
A broken pen-knife, piles of fluff,
And a crumpled handkerchief,

A packet of seeds, the name rubbed out,
And a carefully pressed leaf
Of his favourite tree, in an envelope
(The leaf, not the tree)
A press-stud and a finger-stall,
And a recipe for mint-tea.

And he says, "That's funny. Is that all?
I was sure I had some cough-drops."

So he bangs his coat against the wall,
Filling the house with breezes.
Clouds of dust soon fill the hall,
And tickle his nose till he sneezes.
He beats and shakes, and flaps and flops,
And swings and spins like a top.
Then he splutters, "Enough! I'll have to stop!"
And he coughs and coughs until he drops.

Geoffrey Summerfield

Before the Beginning

Sometimes in dreams I imagine
Alone and unafraid
I'm standing in the darkness
When the first bright stars were made.

When the sun sprang out of the blackness
And lit the world's first dawn
When torrents of rock rained upwards
And the mountains and seas were born.

And I'm there when the forests and meadows
Flowered for the very first time
When eyeless legless creatures
Oozed upwards out of the slime.

But when I awake and read the books
Though they tell me more and more
The one thing they never tell me
Is – what was there before …

Gareth Owen

What She Did

What she did
was really awful
It made me feel quite ill
It was wrong and quite unlawful
I feel queasy still.

What she did
was quite uncalled for
How could she be so cruel?
My friends were all appalled, for
she made me look a fool.

What she did
was out of order
It made me blush and wince
From that instant I ignored her
and haven't spoken since.

What she did
was really rotten.
But what it was
I've quite forgotten.

Roger McGough

Mistaken Identity

It wasn't me
Who came in late,
Who slammed the door,
Who slept so long,
Who got it wrong,
Who wanted more,
Who had to wait.
It wasn't me.

It wasn't you
Who shrank from touch,
Who cried all night,
Who rang the school,
Who felt a fool,
Who looked a sight,
Who drank too much.
It wasn't you.

It wasn't us
Who smiled in vain,
Who built the wall,
Who piled each stone,
Who ate alone,
Who bore the pain,
Who lost it all.
It wasn't us.

John Mole

A Fishy Poem

I have nine guppies
there were ten but the mother died shortly
after the birth
the father runs up and down the aquarium
looking

at first I thought I wasn't feeding
them enough
so I increased and increased
until the aquarium was very very dirty
then I realized he was just a guppie
whose father was a goldfish
and he was only following
his nature

Nikki Giovanni

Visiting Rights

Sarah asks her Mum if she can
come to my place, just for the afternoon,
and her Mum, quick as a flash, says,
"Certainly, as soon as you clean your room."
Peter's Mum is the same,
"Yes Peter, you can go, but only after you've
picked up all the empty potato crisp wrappers from
your room, and put them where they belong."
Li's Mum says,
"Yes, but first I want all the toys collected
from the backyard. It looks like a toy dump."
Penny's Dad says,
"Well ... OK. But would you mind making
your bed first?"
Matthew's Mum always says,
"Of course you may Matthew. As soon as your
homework is done."

But there are some unpredictable parents.
Sam asks if he can come over and his Mum says,
"Sure. Stay the night if you want. See you tomorrow."
And when Rebecca asks her Mum, Mrs Lester says,
"You can visit that kid when the cows come home."

Rebecca doesn't have any cows.

Steven Herrick

El Garrobo

*El gran garrobo lapo
que vivía en la cumbrita
del palo de ojoche
y que se confundía siempre
entre sus hojas,
al fin lo pude coger
y mañana
lo comeremos
en rico pinol.*

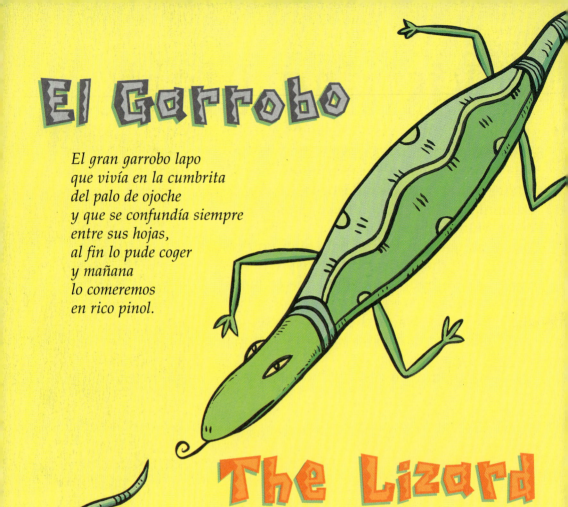

The Lizard

There was a big green lizard
that lived at the very top
of the *ojoche* tree
and was invisible among its leaves.
At last I have been able to catch it
and tomorrow
we shall eat it
in a tasty stew.

Bosco Centeno

voice in the night

I listen, listen
as I lie in bed.

should I pull the
  covers
over my head?

if I do
then I won't
be able to hear
what it is
that's creeping
near
and nearer
to the house

a ghostly horror
in the night
slithering
slodging
right
beneath my window

but if I don't
hide safe
beneath the sheet
then I'll see it
slothering
over the street

come gaping
in my room
with a ghastly grin

ghoulish-white
gaunt and thin

eyes gleaming red
as bloody pools
glaring inside
black mouth wide
a moor-bleak cave
sharp fangs raise
it's wanting to
hoping to
ready to
taste my blood

I shiver alone
scream silently
wonder why
the vampire
has chosen me

take my fingers
from my ears
as hot tears rise
slide down my cheeks

and hear
a voice outside
crying
out of the darkness
soft
and urgently
*Let me in, our kid,
I've lost my key!*

Joan Poulson

I Want to Forget

I want to forget
But I cannot forget.
I do not see him
But I am devoted to him.
Even when I sleep
I repeat his name.
When I walk in the streets
I stare at the people
And I feel like crying
If they do not mention his name …

The Rebel Poet-Priest of Bengal

A Game of Squash

If there's one thing that's worse than a Headlouse,
Then it must, I suppose, be a Bedlouse.
But as I've understood lice
(And excepting the Woodlice),
Why, the only good louse is a dead louse.

Dick King-Smith

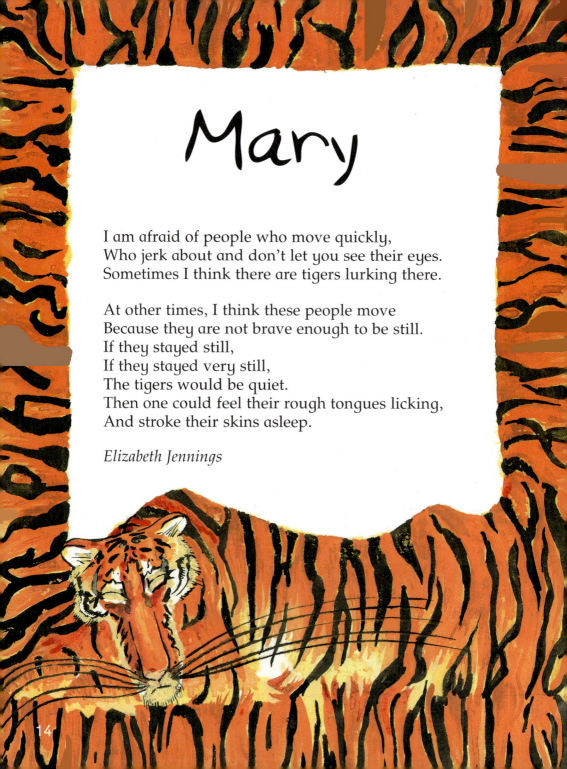

Mary

I am afraid of people who move quickly,
Who jerk about and don't let you see their eyes.
Sometimes I think there are tigers lurking there.

At other times, I think these people move
Because they are not brave enough to be still.
If they stayed still,
If they stayed very still,
The tigers would be quiet.
Then one could feel their rough tongues licking,
And stroke their skins asleep.

Elizabeth Jennings

The Wedding Feast

My sister is the bride today.
I carried the ring into the church
and scattered rose petals on the way out.
Yesterday she chased our peacock
all around the yard
before she plucked
one of its tail feathers for my hat.
I wish I could have brought
my friend to the wedding –
I wanted her to see me in my
new dress, best apron and fancy hat.
They said I'm allowed to stay up
until the dancing is almost over.
It isn't fair that I have to sit
on the floor and get all dusty.
I've hidden a few pieces of cake
in a secret pocket for my friend.
From now on, I have a room to myself
and my sister's husband will have to listen
to all her bossy blather – not me!

Julie O'Callagan

So So Illogical

I am so
illogical I cannot
stand myself!
I allowed the half inch
spider to move nine
stones of me to sleep
next door.
It was surprising how
little it had to say –
being there was plenty.

Sharon Bell

When

Daddy
left us,
he left his
bedroom slippers
beneath the sink
on the bathroom floor.

When
Mama put them
in the giveaway bag
for the poor,
I knew
this time
Daddy
had gone
out the door
for good.

I never
understood
why
he went away
but
every
night
I pray
that
the daddy
who gets
to wear
his slippers
will be kinder
to his family
than Daddy
was to us –

to me.

He has to be.

He
has
to
be.

Lee Bennett Hopkins

Away Day

They never win when I go. Why?
I don't know. But every time
it's the same. A great game and then,
one down five minutes from the end.
My mates say I bring them bad luck,
so now I'm stuck: to go or not to go,
what do I do next? Just give up
and watch the teletext?
They're home today.
I think I'll give them a chance,
and stay away.

Adrian Henri

Just Wait

Ah goin' to live in a de forest,
Just meself an' me,
Ah goin' to run away when it get light,
Just you wait an' see.

Nobody goin' be there to tell me
Not to paint me toenail red,
Which dress, or blouse, or skirt to wear,
Or what time to go to bed.

Nobody goin' be there to criticise,
Ah goin' be on me own,
Nobody to frown an' make a fuss,
To groan an' gripe an' moan.

Me chair goin' to be a tree stump,
Me bed, banana trash,
Ah goin' eat me food out o' cocoa leaf,
Drink from a calabash.

Ah goin' brush me teeth with chew stick,
An' wash me face with dew,
Ah goin' use withes to make ribbon,
An' coconut husk make shoes.

Ah goin' swim like turtle in the river,
Swing from the highes' tree,
In fact, ah think ah goin' go right now.

But first, let me see what on TV.

Valerie Bloom

All You Who Sleep Tonight

All you who sleep tonight
Far from the ones you love,
No hand to left or right,
And emptiness above –

Know that you aren't alone.
The whole world shares your tears,
Some for two nights or one,
And some for all their years.

Vikram Seth

Something He Left

An overcoat warming a clothes-hanger,
Alone in a cupboard after his body had gone
To be made into flame and memory,
Standing as still as he placed it,
Or very faintly trembling,
The night before the dawn he put death on.

Kit Wright

When I Was a Boy

When I was a boy
On the Isle of Wight
We all had a bath
On Friday night.
The bath was made
Of Cornish tin
And when one got out
Another got in.
    First there was Jenny
    Then there was Jean,
    Then there was Bessie
    Skinny as a bean,
    Then there was Peter,
    Then there was Paul,
    And I was the very last
    One of all.

When mammy boiled the water
We all felt blue
And we lined up like
A cinema queue.
We never had time
To bob or blush
When she went to work
With the scrubbing brush.
    First there was Jenny
    Then there was Jean,
    Then there was Bessie
    Skinny as a bean,
    Then there was Peter,
    Then there was Paul,
    And I was the very last
    One of all.

When I was a boy
On the Isle of Wight
My mammy went to work
Like dynamite:
Soap on the ceiling,
Water on the floor,
Mammy put the kettle on
And boil some more!
    First there was Jenny
    Then there was Jean,
    Then there was Bessie
    Skinny as a bean,
    Then there was Peter,
    Then there was Paul,
    And I was the very last
    One of all.

Charles Causley

ILL

I rather like being ill –
not *terribly* ill, but just a little bit ill,
lying in bed all warm and cosy,
after a tummy-ache or a chill!

The most pleasing thing about it
that I could mention
is that I'm the centre
of attention!

Gavin Ewart

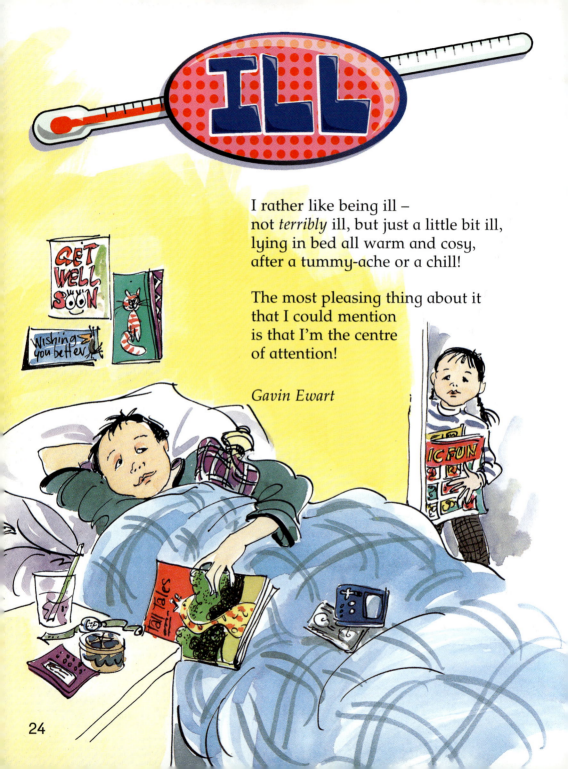

The Pedlar's Caravan

I wish I lived in a caravan,
With a horse to drive, like a pedlar-man!
Where he comes from nobody knows,
Or where he goes to, but on he goes!

His caravan has windows two,
And a chimney of tin, that the smoke
  comes through;
He has a wife, with a baby brown,
And they go riding from town to town.

Chairs to mend, and delf to sell!
He clashes the basins like a bell;
Tea-trays, baskets ranged in order,
Plates, with alphabets round the border!

The roads are brown, and the sea is green,
But his house is like a bathing-machine;
The world is round, and he can ride,
Rumble and slash, to the other side!

With the pedlar-man I should like to roam,
And write a book when I came home;
All the people would read my book,
Just like the Travels of Captain Cook!

William Brighty Rands

You Try to Tell Them

You try to tell them
  What happened
    But they
      don't
        listen,

Then
  they
 find out
     what happened.
   then you
      get all
          the
            blame.

Marisa Horsford

Something to Worry About

Nothing rhymes wid **nothing**
I discovered dat today
Now I hav two more words
To help me rhyme away,
Nothing + **nothing** = **nothing**
I am good at maths as well
I feel like a professor
As me head begins to swell.

If I start wid **nothing**
I hav **nothing** to lose
And now dat I hav two **nothings**
It's easier to choose,
Nothing gets me worried
I hope you overstand
I am now enjoying **nothing**
And I hav **nothing** planned.

I am busy doing **nothing**
Me parents think it's great
I am in luv wid **nothing**
And there's **nothing** dat I hate,
I will give you **nothing**
So you hav **nothing** to fear
Let me tell you **nothing**
I hav **nothing** to declare.

Nothing's rong wid **nothing**
It's such a great idea
It need not be created
I hav **nothing** to share,
Nothing rhymes wid **nothing**
There waz **nothing** at de start
And I can't give you anything
When there's **nothing** in my heart.

Benjamin Zephaniah

Gutted

These flats. I'm getting out of here. I'm not
going to be one of those they come round
collecting for wreaths for.

I want a room of my own. Sean even
gets hold of my underpants if I don't
watch him. And I'm sick of his City posters.

Telly's rubbish in the day. The adverts are
alright. I want to spear a dummy with
a bayonet. I bet my Dad was in the army.
I bet he had boots and a gun.
I would stand to attention. I would
salute with my hand like this.

I wish I wasn't the eldest. Sometimes
I go to the fridge and drink the
baby's milk from her bottle.

Chrissie Gittins

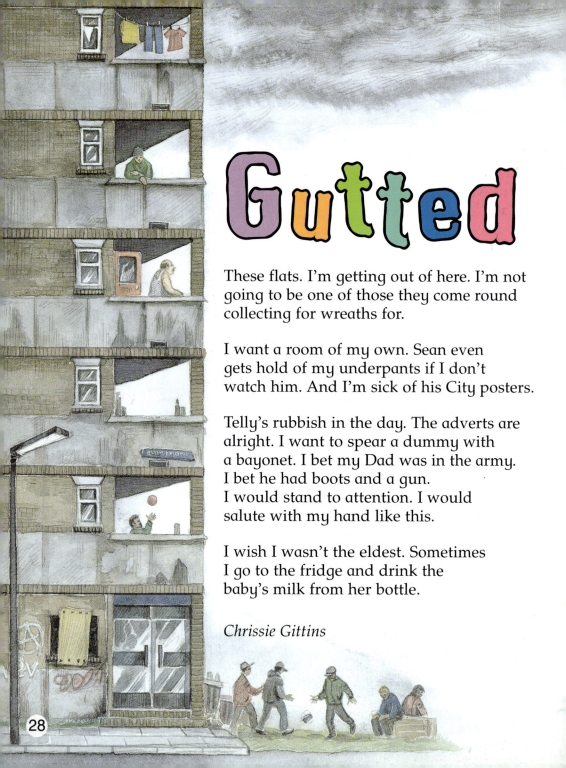

Jealousy

"Who lived in the empty house,
    Behind that door?"
"A widow, and her son
    Back from the war."

"What did he bring with him?
    Did he come alone?"
"He brought his girl; his mother
    Sent her home."

"He took her away? From the
    jealous
    House he fled?"
"He stayed, was ill; five years
    He lay in bed."

"Who came to visit him?
    Who crossed the floor?"
"Except his mother, no-
    body he saw –
    No doctor,
    Nurse,
    Priest,
    Man,
    Woman,
    Or child;
For if they came, his mother
    Stood in the door."

"What of the girl? Was there
    nothing
    She could do?"
"She told their story, and tells it
    Now to you."

Ian Serraillier

Growing Pains

Mother got mad at me tonight and bawled me out.
She said I was lazy and self-centred.
She said my room was a pigsty.
She said she was sick and tired of forever nagging
 but I gave her no choice.
She went on and on until I began to cry.
I hate crying in front of people. It was horrible.

I got away, though, and went to bed and it was over.
I knew things would be okay in the morning;
Stiff with being sorry, too polite, but okay.
I was glad to be by myself.

Then she came to my room and apologised.
She explained, too.
Things had gone wrong all day at the store.
She hadn't had a letter from my sister
    and she was worried.
Dad had also done something to hurt her.
She even told me about that.
Then *she* cried.
I kept saying, "It's all right. Don't worry."
And wishing she'd stop.

I'm just a kid.
I can forgive her getting mad at me. That's easy.
But her sadness …
I don't know what to do with her sadness.
I yell at her often, "You don't understand me!"
But I don't want to have to understand her.
That's expecting too much.

Jean Little

Index of poem features

Ballad 29

Chorus 22, 23

Dramatic monologue 11, 15

Free verse 3, 8, 9, 10, 11, 14, 15, 16, 17, 18, 26, 28, 30

Lament 12
Limerick 13
Lyric 3, 5, 6, 7, 8, 9, 10, 11, 14, 16, 17, 18, 19, 21, 24, 25, 26, 28, 30

Narrative verse 4

Performance poem 2, 27
Prayer 20

Quatrains 5, 25

Rap 27

Song 19, 22